Prince Harry

Prince Harry

Alison Gauntlett

Photographs by the
Daily Mail

p

For Ian, Alice and Matthew

This is a Parragon Book
First published in 2003

Parragon
Queen Street House
4 Queen Street
Bath, BA1 IHE, UK

Produced by Atlantic Publishing Ltd
Origination by Croxons PrePress
Designed by John Dunne

A catalogue record for this book is available from the British Library.

ISBN 1-40540-311-X

Printed in China

Introduction

Prince Harry came of age on 15th September 2002. The second son of Prince Charles and Princess Diana, he is currently third in line to the throne, although this position will change if his older brother William has any children. His mother was always determined that he would never have to play second fiddle to William and the boys have a strong relationship born out of mutual trust and respect.

Following the same educational path as his brother, attending schools specifically selected by his parents for their ethos and ability to give the boys as normal an upbringing as possible, gave Harry the chance to grow in a happy and secure environment. He has matured away from the eyes of the media, mixing with friends he was able to choose for himself.

An intelligent young man with a very quick wit, he is also a daring and talented sportsman who at times seems completely without fear. He is very down-to-earth and this, combined with the communication skills he inherited from his mother, means that he has embraced the opportunities to meet people from all walks of life in his official role.

Harry was totally devastated by his mother's untimely death, two weeks before his thirteenth birthday. He adored his mother and had been very protective towards her when his parents' marriage had broken down. Nobody will forget the sight of the small figure following behind his mother's coffin. After the funeral, it was the security of his family and the stability of his life at Ludgrove that helped him face up to the future. The bond between Harry, William and their father strengthened even further from that day. He still misses Diana dreadfully but is determined to keep her memory very much alive.

A gap year will follow his 'A' level studies at Eton. Like his brother William before him, he will use the opportunity to travel and undertake some charity-based work. He may then head either towards university or the armed forces – that will be a decision for him to make.

Harry marked his eighteenth birthday by carrying out his first charity engagements in memory of his mother. He is very proud of the work she did and is determined to carry on with the things Diana didn't get a chance to finish. At the moment, his studies limit the commitment he can make but he will doubtless increase his charity work in the future. It is clear from what he has done so far that, like his mother before him, he will be very good at it.

Packed with more than 150 photographs from the archives of the *Daily Mail*, many of which have never been published, this book captures the first 18 years in the life of a remarkable young man.

Prince Harry

Prince Henry Charles Albert David came into the world on 15th September 1984. Everyone had waited all day to hear news of the second child due to Prince Charles and Princess Diana and there was much celebration that evening. He was to be known as Harry. Carolyn Bartholomew, a friend of his mother and his godmother, described baby Harry as 'affectionate, demonstrative and huggable'.

Diana was initially worried that older brother William would be jealous of his new sibling. However, she quickly realised that her fears were unfounded. William adored his younger brother at first sight and that strong bond between them has remained ever since.

She also was determined that her son would never be treated any differently, knowing that William was automatically next in line to the throne after Prince Charles. Harry was third in line but that position would change immediately if William were to have any children in the future. The press soon commented that Diana had produced 'an heir and a spare'.

As with his older brother William, his parents wanted to ensure that Harry would lead as normal a life as possible and they also planned that he would follow the same educational path as his brother. Harry's early days were spent mainly at Highgrove and he was initially looked after by a nanny. His parents spent as much time with the two boys as they could and delighted in taking over meal times and bathing their children. However, his parents' marriage was in trouble and by the time Harry was three, Charles was spending most of his time at Highgrove while Diana stayed at Kensington Palace, their London home.

The day after his third birthday, Harry began to attend Miss Mynors' kindergarten in Notting Hill. His parents had chosen this happy and popular school to enable him to mix with other children and enjoy the informal pre-school curriculum offered. He then joined William at Wetherby School when he was five. Harry was quickly assessed as being highly intelligent and demonstrated a love of learning.

He only saw his father at weekends when the family would travel down to Gloucestershire. It was during this time that Diana started taking the boys out for day trips. She would ensure they dressed in jeans and trainers and had the opportunity to take part in activities in the way that any other child would. This included queuing for rides and refusing any preferential treatment.

Harry joined William at Ludgrove in September 1992, when he was eight years old. He had already shown great aptitude and interest in sport and the outdoors and it was fully expected that he would thrive on the curriculum offered at the prep school. However, in December, he and William were called into the Headmaster's office, where Diana quietly explained that she and Charles would be officially separating. In many ways, it was a blessing that he was now at Ludgrove with William – they had each other for company and they were protected from all the media speculation.

When Harry was nine, Tiggy Legge-Bourke became an important part of his life. Charles had employed her, intending that she look after the boys whenever they stayed with him, and Harry was devoted to her. Tiggy was talented at countless sports, good at country pursuits and was great fun to be with. She genuinely cared

for the boys and was there as a friend but also someone they could confide in when they needed. She was a good match for Harry's highly competitive nature and they would spend hours trying to outdo each other!

Harry's life collapsed, when on Sunday 31 August 1997 he was woken by his father at Balmoral to be told that his mother had been killed in the early hours of the morning. Charles had been up most of the night waiting to hear whether she had survived the car crash in Paris and dreaded having to tell the two boys. It was two weeks before Harry's thirteenth birthday. The whole country came to a standstill that day as television reports showed Harry and William being driven to Crathie Church for the Sunday service – he and William had both chosen to attend. Tiggy

immediately flew up to be with them and Harry spent hours talking about the events surrounding the accident and reading the thousands of letters of condolences that poured in by the hour.

All eyes were on Harry's small frame, dwarfed by the four other men in the family who walked in the funeral procession. His card on her coffin marked simply 'Mummy' will never be forgotten – the hearts of the nation went out to this young boy who had lost his mother in a cruel twist of fate just days before he became a teenager. After the burial at the Althorp Estate, he returned to Highgrove to be with Charles, William and Tiggy and spent hours walking and talking about his mother, her life, her death and the future. Eventually he returned to Ludgrove where he was to spend another year.

In 1998, he fulfilled one of Diana's dreams by passing the Common Entrance examination to take up a place at Eton that autumn. He began at the school just before his fourteenth birthday, joining William at Manor House. Here, he was able to indulge in his passion for sport and soon excelled at many competitive team games including the famous Eton 'Wall Game' – a sport not for the faint-hearted.

Harry has grown into a down-to-earth young man who makes friends easily and has a good relationship with his peers. He supports Arsenal and is never happier than when cheering on his football team or shouting for the England rugby team at Twickenham. He is a fearless sportsman and a very capable skier and polo player – now outstripping his father's performance. He is renowned in

the Royal Family for his wit and sense of humour. One member of the Royal Household said 'Harry is a real flirt, absolutely charming and great fun'.

He continues to have great bond with his older brother and there is no sense of envy of William's future role in life. Harry has inherited his mother's communication skills and has already demonstrated a true sense of compassion for others and the ability to talk to people from all walks of life.

As part of the celebration of his eighteenth birthday in 2002 he chose to embark on some charity work. He revealed that his mission in life was to keep Diana's memory alive and to continue her uncompleted work. In a birthday interview he stated that he wanted to 'carry on the things she didn't quite finish'. He is very proud of the work she did. His first solo engagements included visits to Great Ormond Street and a little-known refuge for abused children in London. He is keen to support the smaller

charities to raise their profile and has already determined that profits from his official birthday photographs will benefit a charity called Merlin – funding healthcare in the Third World. Studies at Eton limit the time he is able to commit to charity work but he intends to increase his support in the future.

Harry is still to decide what the next few years will hold. He is intent on taking a gap year where he can travel and be involved in charitable projects. From an early age he had a fascination with the military and so is tempted by spending time in the armed forces. However, he is also interested in taking a degree. He still has time to make a decision but whatever he chooses he will always have the support of his family and the fabulous legacy left to him by his mother.

Prince Harry

Welcome Prince Harry

Prince Harry was born on 15th September 1984. His mother, Princess Diana, had been resting at Windsor Castle when her labour pains began eleven days earlier than expected. She was immediately taken to the private Lindo Wing of St Mary's Hospital in Paddington at 7.30 am. News of her arrival at the hospital soon spread and the press very quickly gathered *(above)*.

He was eventually born at 4.20 pm, weighed 6 pounds 14 ounces, had light blue eyes and reddish hair. Charles and Diana were anxious that his older brother William should see him as quickly as possible. The following day, two-year-old William arrived at the hospital at 9.00 am and raced down the corridor to find his mother and Harry. He was entranced by his baby brother.

Prince Charles and Princess Diana left the hospital in the afternoon and returned to Kensington Palace *(right)*. While Harry slept, the country celebrated. At Heathrow airport sticks of rock were given to passengers and postcards showing a cartoon of Concorde with a baby's cot hanging from its nose!

Opposite: When Harry was six months old, the family travelled to Balmoral for the start of their Easter holiday. William made the journey separately with his nanny Barbara Barnes. It was policy that the two boys would never travel together by air.

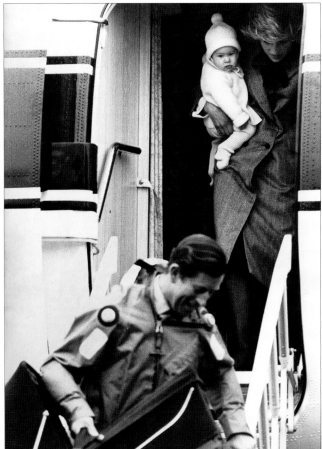

Henry Charles Albert David

Shortly after his birth, Princess Diana wrote to a friend, 'William adores his little brother and spends the entire time pouring an endless supply of hugs and kisses on Harry, and we are hardly allowed near. I can't quite believe I am now a mother of two.'

Harry was christened Henry Charles Albert David on 21st December at St George's Chapel, Windsor Castle. His godparents were Lady Celia Vestey, Lady Sarah Armstrong-Jones, Carolyn Bartholomew (Diana's former flatmate), Prince Andrew, Bryan Organ (royal artist) and Gerald Ward.

Opposite and above: Harry reluctantly descends the steps of the Andover plane of the Queen's Flight.

Early Days

In his early days Harry lived mainly at Highgrove, while also spending time at Kensington Palace, the family's London residence. The Duchy of Cornwall purchased Highgrove in 1980 to be used as the family's private country house. Set in 900 acres of land it was run as a commercial enterprise and the space gave Harry and William the freedom to run and play in their early years. In the walled garden Harry would sit for hours digging holes with his miniature garden tools while Charles worked alongside.

Above and left: Harry surveys the scenes at Aberdeen airport. He was eighteen months old.

Opposite: Harry watches his father play polo at Cirencester Park in Gloucestershire.

Harry's Interests

From a very early age, Harry showed a great interest in anything military in nature. He collected toy lead soldiers and built up a collection of military memorabilia. It was combined with a very early interest in history. Once he was able to read he constantly studied books on the Henrys in the Royal Family. His greatest love was the Parachute Regiment and he always told his parents that this was what he wanted to do when he grew up.

At this early age Harry worshipped his brother William. Harry would copy everything he did and in return William would always play the role of the protective older brother.

Opposite and above: Harry at Smith's Lawn, Windsor.

Nanny 'Roof'

Opposite below right: Harry with his nanny Ruth Wallace. For the first two years of his life he was looked after by Barbara Barnes. However, in January 1987, she left royal employment and was replaced by Ruth Wallace whom the boys soon called Nanny 'Roof'. She was a very brisk and businesslike woman who had a great amount of experience with children. She previously worked for the family of ex-King Constantine of Greece. She quickly endeared herself to the staff at Highgrove and had been given permission by Diana to smack the boys if the need arose.

Opposite top left and right: Watching Prince Charles play polo was a regular event although on this occasion, refreshments and offering polo ponies sugar lumps held more appeal to Harry than the match!

Opposite below left: Harry playing in a stream at Balmoral – he was two and a half.

Above: Just before his third birthday the family stayed with the King of Spain at Palma in Majorca. During a photo call a fight had begun between the King's dogs and Harry was quick to cuddle Perros, the Queen's longhaired lapdog.

Miss Mynors' Kindergarten

In September 1987, the day after his third birthday, Harry followed in his brother's footsteps and began at Miss Mynors' kindergarten in Notting Hill. In the car he was reported to be reluctant to go but once he saw the waiting press he immediately started larking around and earned the nickname 'Harry, the Clown Prince'. He spent the first day making a pair of binoculars out of two toilet rolls. He was to spend two mornings a week there and initially took a while to settle in but soon made friends and emerged as a natural leader in the playground.

Above right: Harry meets his new Headmistress, Miss Jane Mynors.

Opposite and above left: Harry and William in Majorca when the family stayed with King Juan Carlos and Queen Sofia.

Left: Harry in Hyde Park by the Serpentine. He had earlier been talking to a fisherman and had asked what maggots were used for.

First Nativity

Opposite below right: Dressed in a pixie hat, green tunic and red tights, Harry played the part of a goblin in his first nativity play. The kindergarten put on a performance of 'The Little Christmas Tree' to parents. There were three classes at the kindergarten. The children began in the Cygnets before moving on to the Little Swans and then the Big Swans. There were twelve children in each class. The children were taught the basics of numbers and letters and there was a great deal of emphasis on creative work. Children were encouraged to use paint and clay regularly.

Opposite top and below left: Harry getting an early introduction to horse riding at Sandringham.

Above: Harry, with Peter and Zara Phillips, climbs aboard a vintage 1936 fire engine on the Sandringham estate.

Kindergarten Days

Opposite top left: Harry arrives with his mother and brother to watch the Royal Tournament.

Opposite top right: Prince Harry on his fourth birthday.

Opposite below left: On his first day back at school after the summer holidays, Harry emerged carrying that morning's handiwork.

Opposite below right: Harry attended William's school Christmas carol concert at the Palace Theatre. William was now at Wetherby School.

Right and below: At Miss Mynors' the children were encouraged to take part in plays and concerts. In December 1988 he played the role of the shepherd in the annual nativity and had a small speaking part. He reportedly relished the applause he was given at the end of the performance.

Christmas Nativity

Opposite: Harry crosses the road to take part in the Christmas nativity. He was with a detective and would have to get used to being accompanied by a member of the royal protection squad.

Above: In 1989 Harry attended the Easter Sunday service at St George's Chapel, Windsor Castle.

Weekly Visits to the Queen

By now Harry and William visited the Queen on a weekly basis. Usually they would see the Queen at her private chambers at Windsor Castle with their detectives and nanny. The visits were informal but were also to prepare the young princes for the lives that they would lead in the future. Harry was able to see first hand the informal relationship the Queen had with her estate workers and the respect she had for them. He has great affection for his grandfather, the Duke of Edinburgh, who despite his gruff and aloof appearance has a great sense of humour and was very popular amongst the staff.

Above: After the Easter Sunday service, Harry left with the Queen.

Opposite: Harry emerges with his mother from the entrance to Wetherby School.

Wetherby School

It was soon time for Harry to begin his pre-prep education and he joined William at Wetherby School in Notting Hill. Resplendent in his new uniform, he began just before his fifth birthday on 11th September 1989, a few days late owing to a viral infection. The school had 140 children and he would attend mornings only until half-term and would be taught in a class of thirty. The school's Headmistress Fredrika Blair-Turner greeted him and he confidently ran up the steps pausing to wave at the assembled cameramen before disappearing in for his first session.

The first morning's curriculum was model-making, construction with educational toys and discussions about the children's weekend activities.

He was considered highly intelligent by his teachers and placed in the top group of students. A member of Charles's staff at the time described Harry as 'a walking encyclopaedia – he positively loved learning new things, any scrap of information interested him as long as it was something new'.

Pageboy to Viscount Althorp

Left and opposite: The day after his fifth birthday Harry was pageboy to his uncle, the Viscount Althorp, at his marriage to Victoria Lockwood. The wedding took place on the Althorp Estate in Northamptonshire.

Below: January 1990. Harry waves to the crowd as he leaves the Sandringham parish church with the Queen and Queen Mother.

Harry and William were now at School together and the bond between them continued to grow. William tended to take the lead and Harry was happy to look to William for guidance and support. Staff at Wetherby School had grown used to having two pupils from the royal family in their midst. Bodyguards constantly followed the boys and made their best efforts to appear inconspicuous, but teachers and pupils alike were also very good at ignoring them by now!

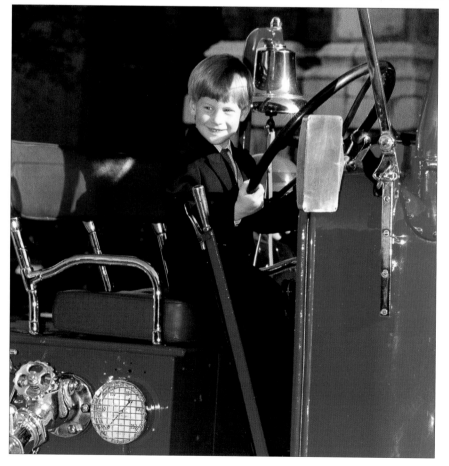

Sixth Birthday Surprise

Above right and opposite: Harry's sixth birthday treat was a visit to the Battle of Britain 50th anniversary exhibition with a group of school friends. Diana had arranged it as a surprise and collected the group of children from school in a coach. During the visit he sat in the cockpit of a Harrier jump jet and was shown how to operate a World War II Bofors anti-aircraft gun. The group returned to Kensington Palace for tea proudly bearing the RAF stickers that they had collected.

Above left: Harry on a family skiing holiday to Lech in Austria.

Left: In October 1990 Harry took part in his first official function. He attended a memorial service at St Paul's Cathedral to the 1,002 fire fighters who died in the Blitz. Afterwards he had the opportunity to climb aboard a restored Leyland Metz fire engine that had been involved in service during World War II.

Solo performance

Opposite: Harry walked in the school crocodile with classmates to the annual school carol service. His mother attended the concert at St. Matthew's church in Bayswater where she proudly listened to him sing a solo. He sang 'How Do We Get To Bethlehem' with another boy and they each sang a solo in the alternating verses. He was six years old.

Left: Leaving St George's Chapel, Windsor after the Easter Sunday service in March 1991.

Below left: Harry took part in a children's gymkhana in June 1991. He competed in the showjumping section and displayed great skill as he took his pony over a series of challenging fences, completing a clear round. Princess Diana proudly presented him with two trophies and a rosette.

Below right: Princess Diana reaches for Harry's hand as they arrive at the Albert Hall for the Mountbatten Festival of Music.

Sports Day at Wetherby School

Right and below: The annual Sports Day in 1991 was held at Richmond Athletic Ground. Harry took part in all his events with great enthusiasm and even had two tries at the sack race. Princess Diana lined up for the mothers' race intent on improving on her second position last year but was again pipped at the post. Prince Charles missed out on the fathers' race as he sat out with crippling back pain.

Opposite top: Harry travelled in an open carriage after the Trooping of the Colour ceremony on Horseguards Parade.

Opposite below left: Harry manfully tugged his suitcase down the steps of the aeroplane at Aberdeen airport. He was joining the rest of the Royal Family for the traditional summer holiday at Balmoral.

Opposite below right: Attending a polo match with his father.

Harry's Seventh Birthday

Left: A special surprise was laid on for Harry for his seventh birthday in the grounds of Kensington Palace. Other people in the park were treated to the sight of Harry whooping with delight at the dog-handler team clowning around with a display of cops-and-robber chases. The dogs were breaking up fights between policemen wielding baseball bats. Cousins Eugenie and Beatrice and a group of school friends joined him.

Below left: The Duchess of York with Eugenie at Harry's birthday celebrations.

Below right: Harry and Princess Diana attended a concert at Wembley given by the massed bands of the household division.

Opposite: On his way to Wetherby carol service - Christmas 1991.

Aptitude for Learning

Harry was nearing the end of his time at Wetherby. The school had provided him with a wide and varied curriculum and given him the chance to excel in the areas in which he showed particular talent, such as the performing arts. He had also demonstrated great aptitude at the computer, by building on the skills he had learnt at home playing games with William and using a variety of CD-roms.

Opposite: Harry holds on tightly to the drag lift while on a skiing holiday at Easter in 1992.

Below left: The princes leave the Natural History Museum holding flowers and chocolate after a visit to the dinosaur exhibition with their mother.

Below right: Harry after the Easter Sunday service.

Right: A Christmas treat: Harry with his mother and William after seeing an opera at the Coliseum in London on Christmas Eve 1992.

Natural Storyteller

Opposite: Harry stood confidently ready to take part in the obstacle race in his last year at Wetherby School but was beaten by the weather. At Richmond Park Athletic Ground Harry skidded and fell on the wet grass finishing third. The rest of the programme was cancelled as the rain cascaded down.

Above and right: Playtime and sports with classmates from Wetherby.

His favourite lessons at Wetherby were art and model-making, but he also liked English. He loved writing stories and his teachers described him as 'gifted'.

Last Days at Wetherby

Opposite and above left: Harry walked to St Matthew's church in Bayswater for the church service that marked his last day at Wetherby School. He walked hand in hand with a school friend holding an order of service book. He was due to join William at Ludgrove Preparatory School in the autumn.

Above right: Harry sees his father leave Kensington Palace by helicopter to carry out the day's public engagements.

Right: Princess Diana took Harry and William to see the Grand Prix at Donington Park. Harry had the chance to try out the latest Williams car.

In December 1992, Charles and Diana separated. The day before an announcement in the House of Commons, Diana travelled down to Ludgrove to tell William and Harry.

High Jinks at Thorpe Park

Opposite: Diana took William and Harry to their favourite theme park at Thorpe Park in Surrey. One of the highlights of the day was the Hudson Rafters Race where the family delightedly came out absolutely soaked. They were accompanied by their detective team but were determined to queue to pay and wait for rides in the same way as everyone else. The highlight for Diana and the boys was watching the detectives getting even wetter in the ride behind them!

Above: More skiing practise for Harry, this time on the slopes at Lech, Austria.

Harry in the Fast Lane

Above left: Princess Diana had bought the boys 60cc go-karts and she took them to Buckmore Park in Kent to try them out. The boys confidently raced them round the 400-yard circuit as their mother watched excitedly. The machines were made by Zipcart, a British company and one of their company spokesmen said, 'They may be princes but today they were just two youngsters having a great day out. They had a terrific time. Both are very keen drivers and show promise.'

Above right and right: Harry at the Guards Polo Club in Windsor Great Park in May 1993, while Prince Charles takes part in a match.

Opposite: Prince Charles won a bottle of champagne and passed it over to Harry to look after. Harry reportedly ripped off his tie in celebration!

Disney World

Below: In August 1993, Diana took the boys to Disney World in Florida. One day was spent at the Disney World MGM theme park. On this occasion, the security measures meant they had to bypass all the queues and other tourists. The highlight of the boys' day was the Indiana Jones Stunt Spectacular where despite an attempt at a discreet entrance, the royal party was given a standing ovation.

Opposite: At Smith's Lawn, Windsor Great Park.

Right: Harry with his mother after watching a performance of *Riverdance*.

During this time, Diana was intent on showing Harry and William a very different side of life to their own. During Ascot Week, she arranged a visit to a refuge night shelter run by nuns for street people. When they arrived she left the boys to make their own introductions and Harry was soon involved in a card game with one man seeking shelter. His mother was then able to talk to him and ensure he understood about the plight of the homeless when they returned to Kensington Palace later that night.

Grand Day at Silverstone

Above and right: In July 1993 Harry had the opportunity to attend the Grand Prix at Silverstone. He went with cousin Peter Phillips and former racing driver Jackie Stewart, who escorted them around the track.

Opposite: He met racing driver Damon Hill and then was invited to sit behind the wheel of a Formula Three car.

When Harry was nine years old, Prince Charles employed Tiggy Legge-Bourke. She was technically an assistant to his private secretary but in reality was to be nanny to Harry and William whenever they were with their father. She quickly became a friend and confidante and would play happily alongside the boys. Tiggy was very talented at many sports and would provide a serious challenge to the boys' competitive natures. She also gave them plenty of affection when they needed it. Harry adored Tiggy and soon became very attached to her.

'Soldier-Mad' Harry

Right and opposite: Harry accompanied Princess Diana on a visit to the Light Dragoons in Germany. Diana was heard to remark that eight-year-old Harry was 'soldier-mad at the moment'. At the beginning of the visit she inspected the troops and he followed behind on his best behaviour, first shaking the hand of a senior officer.

Formalities over, he then spent the day with Lieutenant David Chubb who took him to get changed and then made sure he had some fun. An army seamstress had cut down a uniform to size and the pocket bore the words 'HRH The Prince'. He clambered aboard a ten-ton Scimitar reconnaissance vehicle with a thirty millimetre cannon. He put on the commander's helmet and radio microphone and was driven to the parade ground where he watched troops fight a mock battle He had a fabulous time and later went home in the royal limousine with his face streaked with camouflage paint.

Below left: Returning from a visit to Scotland in the autumn of 1993.

Below right: Harry on his way to Sticky Fingers restaurant, owned by Rolling Stone, Bill Wyman, for a meal with his mother and William.

Confidence With The Public

Right: On a visit to the Horse of the Year Show, Harry was seen emulating his father's mannerisms as he walked around with one hand in a pocket. At the age of nine he was clearly showing that he could deal with social functions with confidence and ease.

Opposite: Harry and William, dressed in jeans and sweatshirts, blend in with the crowd on the 'Nemesis' ride at Alton Towers, Easter 1994. Eleven-year-old William had his doubts at first, eventually being persuaded to take the plunge by his nine-year-old brother. William was glad of Harry's insistence - the high-flying Princes enjoyed the ride three times in all!

Below: In a change of mood and attire, Harry and William on official duty wave to the gathered crowds.

Out and About

Opposite: Harry happily leaves a sweet shop with his mother.

Below left: Leaving the Chicago Rib Shack, Knightsbridge, with his brother, William, close behind.

Left: Prince Harry was already showing a great talent for skiing and in February 1994 he accompanied his father to Klosters. As they travelled up the Gotschna mountain they passed the scene where Prince Charles narrowly escaped death in an avalanche but where Major Hugh Lindsay, former equerry to the Queen, was killed.

Below right: Already an accomplished rider, Harry took part in the Beaufort Hunt when he was eleven.

Home and Away

Below and right: On a visit to Duku Duku in South Africa, Charles and Harry took time out to watch some Zulu dancing.

Opposite left: Harry at Clarence House for the Queen Mother's 97th birthday celebrations.

Opposite right: On holiday with Charles at Klosters. After many skiing holidays Harry had become a very confident and able skier.

Balmoral

Opposite above left: Harry snowboarding on the slopes at Klosters. He had suffered a fall thirty-six hours earlier but was soon back on the runs, sporting a fading black eye.

Opposite above right: Arriving at the Pacific Space Center in Vancouver when on holiday with Charles and William.

Above and opposite below: At Polvier by the River Dee in Scotland. It was near the end of this summer holiday that Harry would hear the tragic news of his mother's death.

Death of the Princess of Wales

Harry was on holiday at Balmoral with William and his father when the news came through that Diana had been killed in a Paris car crash. He was woken on the morning of 31 August 1997 to be told the news by Prince Charles. It was a fortnight before his thirteenth birthday. Tiggy immediately flew up to Scotland to be with them. Charles was particularly protective of his younger son throughout the harrowing day of Diana's funeral.

Diana's Funeral Procession

Harry followed the funeral cortège alongside William, Charles, the Duke of Edinburgh and Earl Spencer. Walking with four tall men, Harry looked so young and vulnerable. His card on Diana's coffin with the word 'Mummy' will always be remembered. Despite his young age, he followed the coffin for a mile to Westminster Abbey, and then sat through the funeral service before travelling to the Althorp Estate in Northamptonshire, where his mother was buried on an island in the middle of a lake. Afterwards, he returned to Highgrove with William and Charles. As well as spending time with them, he spent hours walking and talking to Tiggy about the events, and poring over the countless messages of condolence.

Family Events

Opposite: Harry walks to Sandringham Church with his father and his cousin Zara Phillips, for the traditional Christmas morning service.

Below: Harry joins other members of the royal family to celebrate the Queen Mother's 98th birthday. Left to right: Duke of York, Princess Beatrice, Prince Charles, Prince Harry, Prince William, The Queen and Prince Edward.

In March 1998 Charles took Harry and William on the royal visit to Canada. The superstar welcome from teenage girls that the two boys received was overwhelming. Harry thoroughly enjoyed the attention that he was given!

Right: At Whistler Ski Resort in Canada.

Harry Joins William at Eton

Opposite: On 2nd September 1998 Harry was driven to Eton College by his father to begin his first day at his new school. He had passed the Common Entrance examination in June and knew that he was fulfilling his mother's wish that both boys should go to Eton. He went into the Manor House – his home for the next five years - and had supper with his housemaster Dr Andrew Gailey. Dr Gailey's wife, the house-matron Elizabeth Heathcote and some of Harry's new housemates joined them with their parents.

Above: Prince Charles and Harry arriving at the Eurostar terminal at Waterloo station, to catch the train to France, to watch England play Colombia in the World Cup.

Christmas at Sandringham

Opposite below: Harry, William and their father after the Christmas service at Sandringham.

Opposite top: Harry with Prince Charles and Zara Phillips at the wedding of Santa Palmer-Tomkinson and writer Simon Sebag-Montefiore. The marriage took place at the Liberal Jewish Synagogue in St John's Wood, North London with the reception at the Ritz Hotel.

Above: The year 1999 began with a family skiing holiday in Klosters.

Happy Holidays

Opposite below: William and Harry having fun off the piste with their father at Klosters. By now both sons were considerably taller than their father. The bond between the boys and Prince Charles had grown stronger since the death of their mother.

Right and opposite top: Harry at Klosters.

Below: At Highgrove, Harry jokes with William and Charles. William had just received his first driving lesson from a police sergeant at the beginning of the princes' summer holidays in July 1999.

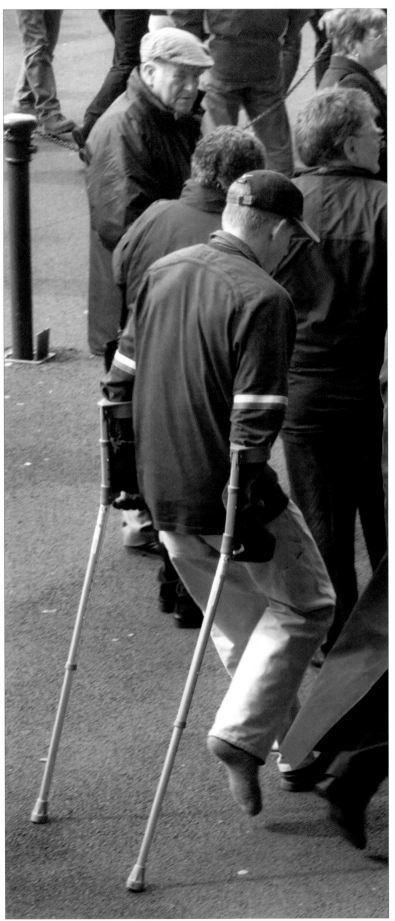

Harry on Crutches

Left: Harry arrived to watch the England v France Six Nations match at Twickenham on crutches. He was sixteen at the time and had been injured at a private party at Highgrove when he accidentally put his foot through a glass door. He would be left with a significant scar.

Opposite top: Harry with Zara Phillips at the Christmas Sandringham Church service.

Opposite below: Harry and William after the service. Their great-grandmother, the Queen Mother, attended the church making her first public appearance since breaking her collarbone two months earlier.

Above: Harry at St George's Chapel, Windsor to celebrate the 80th birthday of the Duke of Edinburgh.

Football Crazy - Rugby Mad

Harry has inherited both his parents' talent for sport and he is a fearless and accomplished player in many different games. He is a very keen footballer and rugby player, and loves both cycling and cricket. He particularly enjoys the 'Wall Game' a sport played only at Eton which is a cross between football and rugby, with very complex rules, involving a great deal of aggression.

Right and below: Wearing an England shirt (Number 10 for Johnny Wilkinson), Harry watched England beat Australia 21 - 15 in the Rugby Union International at Twickenham.

Opposite top and below: Harry at the Six Nations rugby, on this occasion watching England beat Wales 50 -10.

Death of the Queen Mother

On 30th March 2002, Harry's great-grandmother passed away after several months of illness, aged 101. At the time Harry and William were on the slopes at Klosters enjoying their annual Easter skiing holiday. They immediately flew back to England to see the staggering response from the British public. Thousands gathered on the streets of London and filed past her coffin as she lay in state in Westminster Hall.

Her funeral was held a week later and she was buried alongside her husband King George VI at St George's Chapel, Windsor.

Above and opposite: Harry, wearing morning dress, follows the coffin of the Queen Mother as the ceremonial procession takes her from the Queen's Chapel to Westminster Hall for the official lying-in-state.

Harry's Polo Victory

Harry took part in a polo match at Hurtwood Park with his father in aid of the Prince's Trust. Polo is another sport in which Harry had come to excel. The Prince's team won the match 8-6.

In January 2002, the media was full of reports that Harry had admitted to his father that he had been drinking and smoking marijuana. It dominated the news for several days. Prince Charles had already responded to Harry's confession by taking him to a drug rehabilitation centre in London where he met recovering addicts. The country applauded the way his father had dealt with a problem experienced by many parents.

Golden Jubilee

In 2002 the country celebrated the fiftieth year of the reign of Queen Elizabeth II. All over the country people held street parties and special events. On 4 June a Thanksgiving Service was held at St Paul's Cathedral. Thousands of people gathered in the streets of London to watch the royal procession and to join in the celebrations afterwards.

Opposite top: Prince Andrew, Prince William and Prince Harry arrive to join the congregation at St Paul's.

Opposite below: Harry left Buckingham Palace to take part in the procession. He travelled with Princess Beatrice.

Left: Harry watched the Jubilee flypast from the balcony at Buckingham Palace with his brother William. It consisted of 27 aircraft including the Red Arrows and Concorde.

Below: Meeting some of the crowds gathered along The Mall.

Coming of Age

On 15th September 2002, Harry celebrated his 18th birthday during his last year at Eton. He marked the event with a series of official engagements. These included a visit to a drop-in centre for abused children in south London and another to Great Ormond Street Hospital. He has inherited his mother's communication skills and spent many hours chatting to young people. Mario Testino, his mother's favourite photographer, took the official birthday photographs. He has decided that profits made from selling the photographs to the media will benefit a charity called Merlin - a UK-based organisation that provides healthcare for people in the Third World.

Opposite: Harry and William leave St Paul's following the Jubilee Thanksgiving Service.

Above: Harry in The Mall with well-wishers.

ACKNOWLEDGEMENTS

The photographs in this book are from the archives of the *Daily Mail*.
Particular thanks to Steve Torrington, Dave Sheppard, Brian Jackson, Alan Pinnock,
Richard Jones and all the staff.

Thanks also to Cliff Salter, Richard Betts,
Peter Wright, Trevor Bunting and Simon Taylor.
Design by John Dunne.